BRAIN-BOOSTING PUZZLES

NUMBERS

Sarah Khan

QED Publishing

Editorial Director: Victoria Garrard
Art Director: Laura Roberts-Jensen
Designers: Austin Taylor and Rosie Levine
Illustrations by Julie Ingham

First published in the UK in 2014 by
QED Publishing
A Quarto Group company
The Old Brewery
6 Blundell Street
London, N7 9BH

www.qed-publishing.co.uk

Rubik and Rubik's Cube and the images
of the Rubik Cube are Trademarks used
under license by Rubik Brand Limited.
www.rubiks.com All other intellectual
property rights reserved.

A catalogue record for this book is
available from the British Library.

ISBN 978 1 78171 564 2

Printed and bound in China

BB

Look out for the
puzzles marked as
Brain Busters –
they're the hardest!

**Picture credits (fc=front cover,
bc=back cover, t=top, b=bottom,
l=left, r=right, c=centre)**

Big Stock: bccl Homestudio
Shutterstock bctc Nick Kinney, 4
Rocket400 Studio, 4 Aratehortua, 6
Marina Koven, 6 Skalapendra, 6 Michael
Roeder, 8 patrimonio designs ltd, 8
Michele Paccione, 9 Portare fortuna, 10c
My Portfolio, 11 Dario Sabljak, 12tl Nick
Kinney, 12c hin255, 12 Yu Lan, 13 KennyK,
13t Oxygen64, 16 MisterElements, 18
Sarawut Padungkwan, 19tr Nick Kinney,
19t mart, 19bl OSIPOV, 19 Diamond_
Images, 22t Nick Kinney, 22l Adam Hicks,
22 Tribalium, 22c Olegro, 23r SONCHAI
JONGPOR, 23t casejustin, 25 Akinina
Olena, 26tl Nick Kinney, 27 Nick Kinney,
28 Doem, 29 notkoo, 30tl Nick Kinney,
30 silver tiger, 30c farmer79, 31tr Nick
Kinney, 31b Santi0103, 31r dedMazay, 31l
dedMazay, 32c white_board, 32 Pasko
Maksim, 33tr Nick Kinney, 34 Monkik, 35
Artisticco, 36 Nataleana, 37 casejustin, 39
kalomirael, 43 Analia26, 43 Zern Liew, 44t
Roman Sotola, 44c Fejas, 46 zzveillust,
47 djem

Contents

KITE FLYING

Which numbers should replace the letters? The answer you get by multiplying the top numbers of a kite is the same as you get by multiplying the bottom numbers.

3 8
6 A

3 4
2
6

6 12
B 9

8 C
4
10

12 5
D
6

LOCKS AND KEYS

Each lock can only be opened by a key with a number that is 25% of the lock's number. Which key will open each lock?

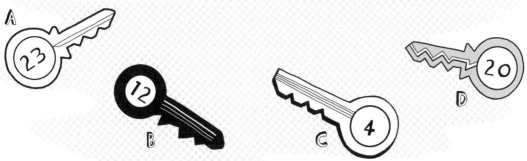

BOW NUMBERS

Which numbers should replace the letters on the bows below? Find the relationship between the numbers on the completed bows to give you a clue.

6

36

9

3

7

A

25

5

C

121

64

B

MOLE MAZE

Help this mole to find its way up through the tunnels to the molehill. What is the sum total of the numbers it passes along the way?

ODD ISLAND OUT

Solve the calculations written
on the sand on each island.
Which is the odd island out?

A

3×4

84 ÷ 7

−5+17   23−11

B

4.5×2   31−2

126 ÷ 14

−4+13

C

4×4   −8+23   48 ÷ 3

53−37

D

3×7   78−57

−3+24   84 ÷ 4

BUNTING NUMBERS

Which numbers should complete each sequence?

A: 10, ?, 22, 28, 34, 40, 46, ?, 58

B: ?9, 92, 85, ?, 71, 64, 57, ?, 43, 36

C: 3, 4, 6, 9, ?, 18, 24, 31, 39, ?

D: 1, 4, 9, 16, 25, 36, 49, 64, ?, ?

IN THE BALANCE

Which white box should you take away to balance the scales so that the totals match on each side?

GOOD EGGS

Old Mother Hubbard needs 6 of the eggs below to make pancakes for all of her children. The eggs marked with a number that is a multiple of 9 have all gone bad. Will she have enough good eggs to make the pancakes?

72

53

36

82

67

18

90

54

34

27

99

63

45

78

108

81

FIND FIFTEEN

Fill in the numbers 1 to 9 in
the grid below so that each
row, column and diagonal
add up to 15. Three numbers
have been filled in for you.

HIGHER OR LOWER?

Which is the highest in each line?
The number of...

1

Ⓐ ...legs on two spiders **OR** Ⓑ ...legs on three elephants.

2

Ⓐ ...hours in three days **OR** Ⓑ ...minutes in two hours.

3

Ⓐ ...wheels on two cars **OR** Ⓑ ...wheels on three tricycles.

4

Ⓐ ...sides on two pentagons **OR** Ⓑ ...sides on three triangles.

5

Ⓐ ...singers in two trios **OR** Ⓑ ...singers in four duos.

WATER SLIDE

The three numbers below are going on the water slide. As they pass through each section of the slide, they'll transform into another number.

Follow the calculation along the sections to find out what each number will be by the time it reaches the bottom of the slide.

3 8 5

×4

÷2

+7

-3

×10

?

CUPCAKE CALCULATION

Betty the baker has made 2 trays of cupcakes identical to the one below. She has to pack the cakes into boxes to take them to a birthday party. She has 9 boxes in total:

2 large ones, which hold 12 cupcakes each,
3 medium ones, which hold 8 each, and
4 small ones, which hold 6 each.

If Betty buys one more box to pack the cakes that are left over, what is the smallest size she will need?

FRIEND OR FOE?

In this alien solar system, the friendly aliens live on the planets with numbers that add up to an even number and the nasty aliens live on the planets with numbers that add up to an odd number. Which of the planets are friendly?

TAKE AWAY TOWER

How long will Rapunzel have to wait before her hair is long enough to reach the prince?

To find the answer, do the calculation down the tower, starting from 100 at the top, and taking away the numbers one at a time. The result is the number of days it will take for her hair to grow down to the prince.

100

-3

-25

-17

-23

-14

-11

PUPPY DAYS

Use the ages below and the following clues to find out which puppy is which:

- Titch is two days older than Dixie.
- Scamp is over twice Mungo's age.
- There is four days' difference between Mungo and Titch.

3 weeks, 3 days

A

1 week, 6 days

B

1 week, 4 days

C

2 weeks, 1 days

D

18

HONEY COMB

Fill the empty cells of this honeycomb with numbers from 1 to 9. The numbers that surround a shaded cell shouldn't repeat and their sum must equal the number in the shaded cell.

SMOOTHIE MAKER

Each smoothie has been made by multiplying one piece of fruit with one type of yogurt. Which fruit and which yogurt haven't been used?

42   15   32

2   7   6   5

4   3   9   8

ON AND OFF

This bus is going from Everdale to Upperton stopping at Riverside on the way. At Everdale there are 7 people on the bus. At Riverside, some people get off the bus and 4 people get on. When it reaches Upperton, there are 9 people on the bus. How many people got off at Riverside?

ARCHERY CONTEST

BRAIN BUSTER!

Three people took part in an archery contest, shooting three arrows each at the target below. Each ring on the target represents points.

Target rings: 10, 20, 30, 40, 50

SCORECARD

Jack	90
David	80
Anna	100

Each contestant shot three arrows and hit three different rings. Their points were added up and written on the scorecard. Counting the different combinations of points they could have scored, in how many ways could each contestant have reached their final score?

CODE BREAKER

12 34 ′ 25

46 21 30 57

8 21 25 25

Secret Agent 770 has received a coded text message telling him the identity of the person who has been selling government secrets to the enemy. Use the information below to decode the message.

31+26 = R	24+22 = Y
25−13 = I	76−42 = T
7x3 = O	5x6 = U
24÷3 = B	125÷5 = S

WITCHES' HATS

The numbers in the shapes on each witch's hat divide exactly into the number on the star at the top. Which numbers are missing from the hats?

27

A
27
?
1   3

B
20
20
10
5
?
2
1

C
14
14
7
?
1

14

18

D
18
9
?   3
2   1

WRITING ON THE WALL

Which numbers should replace the letters? Each number is the sum of the two directly above it.

```
1    4    2    5    A
  5    B    7    8
    11    C    15
      24    D
        E
```

FLOWER POWER

The number in each flower's middle is made by adding and subtracting the numbers on its petals in a particular order. Find the order to calculate the number that is missing from the bottom flower.

26

There are **48** people sitting in the front three rows of this hall. There is a total of **22** people in row A and B, and a total of **36** people in row B and C. How many people are there in each row?

RUSSIAN DOLLS

There are three Russian dolls in each set – one big, one medium and one small. The number on the smallest doll in a set is half the number on the middle doll, which is half the number on the biggest doll. Which two dolls are missing the third of their set?

TEAM NUMBERS

In this team line-up, the numbers on the players' shirts have something in common. Find out what that is, then choose which of the players in the goal below should join the team based on the number on his shirt.

CROSS NUMBERS

How can the numbers 1 to 6 be placed in each cross so that each line of the cross adds up to the number in the circle above it? Some numbers have been placed for you.

11

12

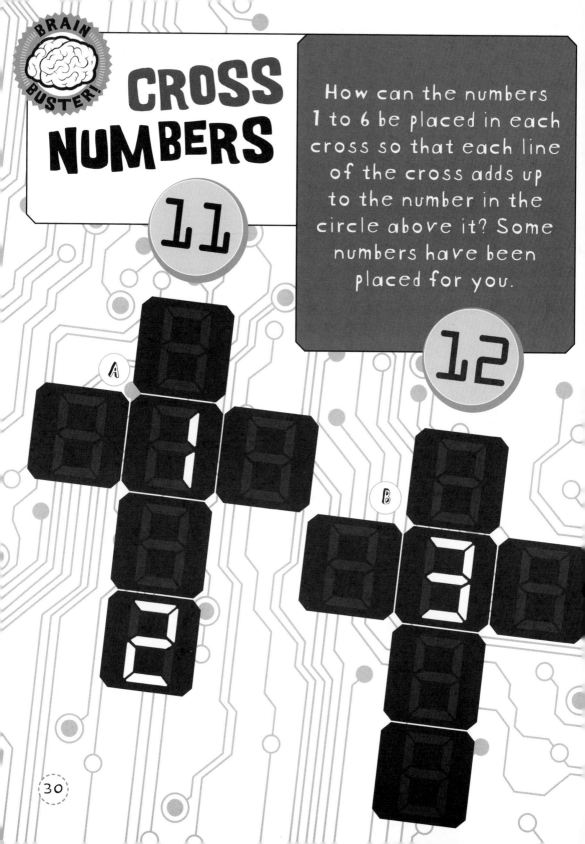

A

B

ROWS AND COLUMNS

The symbols in the grid below stand for the numbers 2, 3, 4 and 5. The numbers around the edge are the sums of the numbers in each row or column. Which symbol represents which number?

				14
				14
				14
				12
15	14	13	12	

31

COUNTING THE DAYS

NOVEMBER

SUNDAY	MONDAY	TUESDAY	WEDNESDAY	THURSDAY	FRIDAY	SATURDAY
			1	2	3	4
5	6	7	8	9	10	11
12	13	14	15	16	17	18
19	20	21	22	23	24	25
26	27	28	29	30		

Amy's birthday is Friday November 17th. What is the date of:

Amy's cousin Sam's birthday which is 12 day before Amy's?

? ? ? ? ?

Sam's friend Joe's birthday, which is 8 days after Sam's?

? ? ? ? ?

Helen's cousin Fred's birthday, which is 9 days after Helen's?

? ? ? ? ?

Joe's auntie Helen's birthday, which is 4 days before Joe's?

? ? ? ? ?

WHAT'S IT WORTH?

The native people of a tiny island in the Indian Ocean don't use money to buy things, but use shells and stones instead.

BRAIN BUSTER!

6 cowrie shells
= 2 jet black stones

4 jet black stones
= 8 clam shells

12 clam shells
= 1 pearl

How many cowrie shells is 1 pearl worth?

jet black stones

clam shells

cowrie shells

pearl

NUMBER CRUNCHER

The Number Cruncher is a machine that takes pairs of numbers and crunches them together to make one number. Look at the number pairs that go into the machine and the number that comes out to find out how each pair has been "crunched".

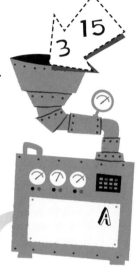

A

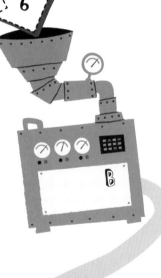

B

C

D

5

13

12

42

Turn these frogs back into princes by finding out which numbers should replace the letters on their crowns. Use these clues to help you:

FROG PRINCES

- Each number in the second jewel is 3 more than the number in the first jewel.

- Each number in the second jewel is half the number in the third jewel.

VEGETABLE PATCH

The vegetables must be picked in numerical order: the vegetable with the lowest value first, and the one with the highest value last.

A) Which vegetable should be picked 5th?

B) Which vegetable should be picked 10th?

Each full jelly bean jar holds 99 jelly beans. The numbers on the shelves show the number of jelly beans that each shelf should hold. How many beans should there be in each empty jar?

JELLY BEAN JARS

A

165

B

224

C

353

FERRIS WHEEL

Starting from the arrow and working clockwise, the numbers on the ferris wheel gondolas are in a sequence. Which numbers should replace the letters?

27   38
A   B
11   66
6   83
3   C
2   123

START

Can you place numbers in the grid so that each row and column add up to the total shown in the arrow? Each number in a row or column must be different.

CROSS SUM

17

18

10

10

9

12

24

8

17

6

5

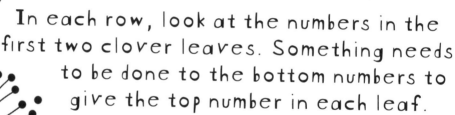

IN CLOVER

In each row, look at the numbers in the first two clover leaves. Something needs to be done to the bottom numbers to give the top number in each leaf. Find out what, then calculate which number should replace the question mark in the last leaf.

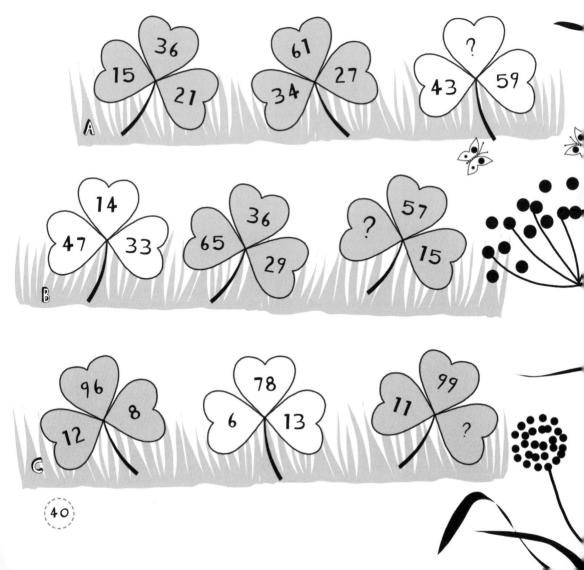

A

Leaf 1: 36, 15, 21
Leaf 2: 61, 34, 27
Leaf 3: ?, 43, 59

B

Leaf 1: 14, 47, 33
Leaf 2: 36, 65, 29
Leaf 3: 57, ?, 15

C

Leaf 1: 96, 12, 8
Leaf 2: 78, 6, 13
Leaf 3: 99, 11, ?

PERFECT PIZZAS

At the Perfect Pizza restaurant, the chef has an order for four different pizzas that all need to be ready at the same time. Take a look at the cooking times for each pizza below. What time should each one go in the oven if they are to be served at 8:15?

A PEPPERONI: 20 minutes to cook

B MUSHROOM & SWEETCORN: 15 minutes to cook

C FOUR CHEESE: 10 minutes to cook

D MEAT FEAST: 25 minutes to cook

PARTY BAGS

Ben made 12 party bags for his birthday party. He numbered them 1 to 12 and put:

a chocolate in every bag with an even number

a bubble tub in every bag with a number that can be divided by three

a sheet of stickers in every bag with a number that can be divided by four.

(A) Which bags contained no gifts?

(B) Did any of the bags contain all three gifts?

BEE HIVES

These three hives are home to
a total of 200 bees. Hive A is home
to 20 fewer bees than Hive B. Hive C
is home to 40 more bees than Hive B.
How many bees live in each hive?

HOOK-A-DUCK

Emma goes to the fair and decides to play the hook-a-duck game. The number on each rubber duck shows how many points she can score for hooking it on the end of a fishing rod.

A
What's the lowest score she can make by hooking three ducks?

B
What's the highest score she can make by hooking three ducks?

C
What's the fewest number of ducks she need to hook to score 20 points?

PIRATE ☠ TREASURE

Pirate Pete and Pirate Penny each have a pile of treasure. Use the key to calculate whose pile is worth more.

Pirate Pete

KEY

60 dubloons

85 dubloons

70 dubloons

55 dubloons

Pirate Penny

TOP TALENT

The votes have been cast for the final
of the TV talent competition, "Top Talent".
Use the information below to find out:
1. the identity of Act 1, Act 2 and Act 3.
2. who won the competition.

Vince the Ventriloquist
received **433,517** more
text votes than the act
with the least amount
of text votes.

The Algerian Acrobats'
total amount of votes
was **1,244,434** fewer
than Dusty the Dancing
Dog's total votes.

	PHONE VOTES	TEXT VOTES
ACT 1	1,234,665	1,576,980
ACT 2	2,008,465	2,010,497
ACT 3	1,960,598	2,095,481

Algerian
Acrobats

Dusty

Vince

How can you put the numbers **4** to **7** in the empty circles so that each straight line of three numbers adds up to **14**?

CIRCLE NUMBERS

1

2

3

Answers

Page 4: A.4, B.8, C.5, D.10

Page 5: 1.C, 2.D, 3.B, 4.A

Page 6: A.49, B.8, C.11

The number on the right side is the number on the left side multiplied by itself.

Page 7: 58

Page 8: C

Each of the other islands have calculations that give the same answer.

Page 9:

A. 16, 52 - add 6 to the previous number.

B. 78, 50 - subtract 7 from the previous number.

C. 13, 48 - the gap between each number increases by 1, so is +1, +2 and so on.

D. 81, 100 - the first flag is 1x1, the second is 2x2, the third is 3x3, and so on.

Page 10: 7

Page 11: No, there are only 5 good eggs - 53, 82, 67, 34 and 78.

Page 12:

8	3	4
1	5	9
6	7	2

Page 13:

1. A - legs on two spiders
2. B - minutes in two hours
3. B - wheels on three tricycles
4. A - sides on two pentagons
5. B - singers in four duos

Page 14:

• 3 will have turned into 100

• 8 will have turned into 200

• 5 will have turned into 140

Page 15: Small

Page 16:

Page 17: 7 days

Page 18: A. Scamp, B. Dixie, C. Mungo, D. Titch

Page 19:

Page 20:

Page 21: 2

Page 22:

• Jack could have made 90 in two ways (10, 30 and 50, or 20, 30 and 40).

• David could have made 80 in two ways (10, 20 and 50, or 10, 30 and 40).

• Anna could have only made 100 in two ways (10, 40 and 50, or 20, 30 and 50).

Page 23: IT'S YOUR BOSS

Page 24: A. 9, B. 4, C. 2, D. 6

Page 25: A. 3, B. 6, C. 13, D. 28, E. 52

Page 26: 15 (8+2−5+7−3+6)

Page 27: A. 12, B. 10, C. 26

Page 28:

Page 29: Number 11

Page 30:

```
          5
      6   1   4       6
          3       5   3   4
          2           2
                      1
```

The numbers can be in different positions within their lines and the answer would still be correct.

Page 31:

Page 32:

• Sam's birthday is Sunday 5th November.

• Joe's birthday is Monday 13th November.

• Helen's birthday is Thursday 9th November.

• Fred's birthday is Saturday 18th November.

Page 33: 18

Page 34: A.÷, B.+, C.−, D.x

Page 35: A.3, B.12, C.10, D.20, E.1, F.4

Page 36: A. 24, B. 62

Page 37: A. 66, B. 26, C. 56

Page 38: A. 18, B. 51, C. 102

The gap between each number goes up by two: 2+1=3, 3+3=6, 6+5=11, and so on.

Page 39:

9	1		
8	9	7	
	8	2	7
		1	5

Page 40: A. 102, B. 72, C. 9

Page 41: A. 7:55, B. 8:00, C. 8:05, D. 7:50

Page 42:

A.1, 5, 7, 11

B.Yes, bag 12

Page 43: A. 40, B. 60, C. 100

Page 44: A. 9, B. 37, C. 2 (12 and 8)

Page 45: Pirate Pete's (Pirate Pete's treasure is worth 610 dubloons, whilst Pirate Penny's is only worth 565 dubloons.)

Page 46:

1. Act 1 is the Algerian Acrobats, Act 2 is Vince the Ventriloquist, and Act 3 is Dusty the Dancing Dog.

2. Dusty the Dancing Dog won the competition.

Page 47:

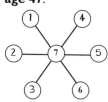